WHY DO ANIMALS HAVE

LEGS and FEET

Elizabeth Miles

Heinemann
LIBRARY

www.heinemann.co.uk/library
Visit our website to find out more information about **Heinemann Library** books.

To order:
 Phone 44 (0) 1865 888066
 Send a fax to 44 (0) 1865 314091
Visit the Heinemann Bookshop at www.heinemann.co.uk/library to browse our catalogue and order online.

First published in Great Britain by Heinemann Library, Halley Court, Jordan Hill, Oxford
OX2 8EJ, a division of Reed Educational and Professional Publishing Ltd. Heinemann is a registered trademark of Reed Educational &
Professional Publishing Limited.

OXFORD MELBOURNE AUCKLAND JOHANNESBURG BLANTYRE
GABORONE IBADAN PORTSMOUTH NH (USA) CHICAGO

Designed by David Oakley@Arnos Design
Originated by Dot Gradations
Printed in Hong Kong

ISBN 0 431 15323 X
06 05 04 03 02
10 9 8 7 6 5 4 3 2 1

British Library Cataloguing in Publication Data

Miles, Elizabeth
   Why do animals have legs and feet
   1.Foot - Juvenile literature 2.leg - Juvenile literature
   3.Physiology - Juvenile literature
   I.Title
   573.9'98'1

Acknowledgements
The Publishers would like to thank the following for permission to reproduce photographs: BBC NHU/Anup Shah p. 25; BBC NHU/Peter Oxford p. 27; BBC NHU/Premaphotos p. 11; BBC NHU/ Flip De Nooyer p. 29; Bruce Coleman Collection/Kim Taylor p. 26; Corbis p. 19; Corbis/Steve Kaufman p. 16; Corbis/Stockmarket Ariel Skelley p. 4; Corbis/Kennan Ward pp. 21, 23; Corbis/Peter Johnson p. 24; Digital Stock p.30; digital vision pp. 14, 15; NHPA/Gerard Lacz p. 9; NHPA/HenryAusloos p. 8; NHPA/Martin Harvey p. 13; NHPA/Mirko Stelzner p. 22; NHPA/Stephen Dalton p. 12; OSF/Tony Tilford p. 20; OSF/David D. Dennis p. 10; OSF/J. A. L. Cooke p. 17; OSF/Jen & Des Bartlett p. 7; OSF/Mark Deeble & Victoria Stone p. 6; OSF/Martyn Colbeck p. 5; OSF/Zig Leszczynski p. 28.

Cover photograph reproduced with permission of Ardea.

Our thanks to Claire Robinson, Head of Visitor Information and Education at London Zoo, for her help in the preparation of this book.

Every effort has been made to contact copyright holders of any material reproduced in this book. Any omissions will be rectified in subsequent printings if notice is given to the Publisher.

Contents

Words in bold, **like this**, are explained
in the Glossary.

Why do animals have legs and feet?

People have legs and feet, and so do many animals. We use our legs and feet for standing up, walking and running. We use them to get from place to place.

Animals have legs and feet of different shapes and sizes. An elephant has thick, sturdy legs and big feet for carrying its huge body. It can run quite fast on its strong legs.

Two long legs

Birds have two legs. Some birds' legs are very long. A flamingo uses its two long legs to stand in the water, while it looks for food.

The ostrich is a bird that cannot fly, but it can run as fast as a car. It can easily escape from **predators**. The ostrich has the longest legs of any bird.

Four legs

Horses have four legs. They can use their legs to **gallop** and jump. Like all legs, horses' legs have **joints** so their legs can bend. Knees and ankles are joints.

A cheetah uses its four, long legs to chase its
prey. The **impala** uses its four legs to run
away. The cheetah is the fastest runner in
the world. Its legs are very powerful.

Lots of legs

Like all **insects**, ants have six legs. These ants use their legs to carry leaves back to their nest. The leaves are heavy for such tiny creatures, but their legs are strong.

Some millipedes are smaller than your smallest finger, but they can have up to 400 legs. A millipede cannot move very fast. It uses its legs to dig through soil.

Jumping legs

Some **insects** have strong back legs for jumping and leaping. A grasshopper can leap between ten and twenty times higher than the height of its own body.

A kangaroo uses its large back legs and feet for high-speed hopping. It jumps up like a spring. A large kangaroo can jump higher than your head, and further than two cars in one bound!

Strong, wide legs

Strong, wide legs can carry heavy weights. A tortoise needs legs like these. It carries its heavy shell on its back wherever it goes. Tortoises' legs move very slowly.

A rhinoceros needs strong, wide legs to carry its heavy body. If it faces danger, its short legs can move fast. The rhinoceros **charges** towards its enemy at high speed.

Legs for swimming

Many animals have legs that are very good for swimming. A frog has powerful back legs. To swim, the frog bends its legs forwards. Then it stretches them back.

A water boatman has strong back legs, too. This **insect** uses them to swim backwards in lakes and ponds. It is called a water boatman because its back legs are like the **oars** on a rowing boat.

Webbed feet

Some animals, like ducks, have **webbed** feet. Their front toes are joined by a web of skin. They use their webbed feet like paddles to help them swim.

An otter has webbed feet for swimming underwater. It uses all four webbed feet to paddle along a river or stream. While swimming underwater it catches fish to eat.

Toes and talons

Parrots have feet with two toes in front and two toes at the back. The toes curl tightly round a branch so that the parrot does not fall. A parrot's toes can also grasp food like nuts.

An osprey has strong toes with curved
talons for grabbing its **prey**. The osprey
dives, feet-first, into a lake or river. It grabs
a fish and carries it off to eat.

Hooves

Some animals walk on their toes. **Hooves** are like strong, hard toenails. A mountain goat's hooves help it to walk safely along steep, rocky slopes.

A reindeer has hooves that protect its toes.
Its spread-out hooves are useful for scraping
away the snow to find plants to eat. They also
help the reindeer to walk in mud and snow.

Feet and legs to dig and kick

Some animals use their feet like digging tools. A green turtle uses its feet like spades. It digs down into the sand to bury its eggs.

Some animals, like zebras, can use their legs and **hooves** for kicking. To defend themselves, and when they fight, zebras kick back their **hind** legs. The animal standing behind may get knocked over.

Feet that grip

A fly has claws and pads on its feet. These grip hard when it lands. The fly can land and walk up a wall without falling off. It can even walk upside down across a ceiling!

A gecko has lots of tiny **ridges** under its feet that help its feet grip very strongly. A gecko can walk up tree trunks and underneath branches. It can walk upside down without falling.

Unusual feet

A starfish has five spiny arms. Underneath the arms are lots of tiny feet. These look like tubes. Suckers on the ends grasp the sea floor as the starfish walks.

A snail's head is on its foot! The foot is the long, soft part under the snail's shell. Slime **oozes** from the foot to help the snail move easily. The snail can put its foot inside its shell.

Fact file

- Legs can only move because of the **muscles** inside. Cheetahs have strong leg muscles, so they can run fast. The fastest cheetah can run as fast as a car.

- When they climb trees, monkeys can grasp branches with their feet as well as their hands. Bats can hang upside down by their feet.

- Feet with claws are called **paws**. Cats and bears have paws.

A grasshopper has powerful back legs for jumping.

Glossary

charges when an animal runs at an enemy to attack it or to frighten it away

gallop the bounding run of horses and zebras

hind a hind leg is a back leg

hooves hard, horny coverings around some animals' toes

impala large African animal, similar to a deer

insect small animal with six legs, and three parts to its body

joints parts of a leg or arm that let it move, like the knee and elbow

muscles parts inside the body that allow people and animals to move

oars long sticks used to push a rowing boat through the water

ooze when a thick liquid comes out slowly

paws animal feet or hands that have claws

predators animals that hunt other animals for food

prey animals hunted as food

ridges parts that stick out from some animals' feet, and help them grip

talons sharp, curved claws

webbed joined by skin

Index

Titles in the *Why Do Animals Have* series include:

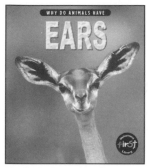

Hardback 0431 15311 6

Hardback 0431 15310 8

Hardback 0431 15326 4

Hardback 0431 15323 X

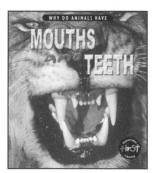

Hardback 0431 15314 0

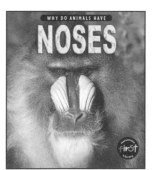

Hardback 0431 15312 4

Hardback 0431 15322 1

Hardback 0431 15325 6

Hardback 0431 15313 2

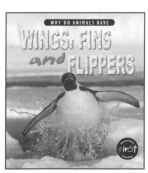

Hardback 0431 15324 8

Find out about the other titles in this series on our website www.heinemann.co.uk/library